IN CASE OF LOSS,
PLEASE RETURN
THIS JOURNAL TO:

....

....

....

....

....

ISBN: 978-1-7371973-1-7
First Edition. Printed in the United States of America Publisher:
Pamela J. Green Solutions, LLC, Washington DC
Editor: Susan Black

MASTERFUL COACH PLAYBOOK & JOURNAL

By Pamela J. Green

HOW TO USE THIS PLAYBOOK AND JOURNAL

This playbook and journal are for professionals who coach, for your own practice and accountability. It is designed as a companion for professionals who, like me, want easily accessible reference prompts, tools, frameworks, structure, and reminders when coaching others.

This playbook and journal is a place for you to make simple notes, access coaching prompts when you get stuck, and serve as a reminder to dance in the moment and remain curious when you're coaching.

I hope you'll find it useful. Let me hear from you on ways to make it even more useful.

WHAT COACHING
IS AND IS NOT

When coaching professionals participate in one of my coach training sessions, they almost always come believing they've always been coaching, and they approach the training as an opportunity to "brush up" on something they've been doing all along.

The truth is they probably have been doing some coaching but have also mixed in some advising, mentoring, counseling and consulting in their conversations. How can you tell? The distinction is in who the coach (that's you) believes has the knowledge about what's best for them (the coachee). If you believe you know what is best and have the answers, then you're not showing up as a coach but instead as an advisor, counselor, mentor, or consultant. If, however, your goal is to help the coachee/client identify and work through what is best for them, not only are you better positioned to coach, but you are teaching them, through your coaching, how to solve their own challenges.

The process of being curious and asking questions for deeper insight, without the attachment to your own ideas on how to solve the challenge, is foundational for every coach, certified or not. If you can't be curious about the client and their situation, then you'll likely find yourself doing something that is not coaching.

I'll provide you with a script and the questions to get started, but will you actually practice detaching yourself from your mindset and perspective to help someone else discover and experience their own? When you do, the questions will flow. Relax, enjoy the conversation and get curious.

COACHING ETHICS

? What standards guide your work?

As a long-time former human resource executive, I too used the term "coaching" to mean performance improvement in the early days of documenting employee performance. While discipline is also considered a form of development used to guide a person's goals, what makes a coaching conversation/relationship different is that if the person doesn't achieve their goals, the risk does not necessarily trigger a company's disciplinary process. Typically, the greatest risk is that the person being coached doesn't achieve their goal at that time. Can the risk be life-threatening, job-threatening, and the like? Of course, but the pressure comes from within and their own desire for growth and development, not because they fear the loss of a job. As a coach, your ethical responsibility is to the client and their goals.

✓ Ethical Guidelines:

• If you are not certified, do not misrepresent yourself, your credentials, or your services.

• Maintain confidentiality. This means in your written notes, casual and formal conversations. Confidential means confidential.

• Acknowledge any conflict of interest. If one emerges during the relationship, know how and when to remove yourself.

• There are a number of people who turn to coaches or establish a coaching relationship for support. You must know how to identify when a person could be better served by another type of professional. If you are not a licensed therapist or otherwise credentialed or certified, you'll need to know how to recognize when these types of services are needed. This is where formal training is important.

• Refrain from offering legal advice if you are not authorized and hired to do so.

COACHING ETHICS

The list goes on and on but knowing and adhering to a set of coaching standards is step one. But what about your own moral sense of right and wrong? Can you make a clear delineation when called to do so?

When you go through a formal coach training program or even attend an ethics session on coaching, you'll learn how to properly handle ethically challenging situations. But if you're uncertain, call your local coach association for additional guidance.

COACHING IS NOT ROCKET SCIENCE

When you're starting out, coaching can feel a bit overwhelming. Resisting the urge to advise and adopting sound listening skills can be challenging. Every coach is challenged from time to time trying to think of the next best question, and even closing a conversation can prove difficult. So, what is getting in the way?

You. Research shows that we are hard-wired in our way of thinking, of seeing the world, and of problem solving. Coaches must remain in the habit of challenging our own assumptions, our tightly held beliefs and biases, and to shift our thinking in ways that allow us to have impactful conversations with our clients.

The three keys to effective and masterful coaching are:

1. A solid foundation.

2. Practice.

3. Accountability.

Let's look at each of these a bit more in depth.

ESTABLISH A SOLID FOUNDATION

Coaching is a framework for the development of others, and some of you will attend a coach training program like mine to learn the skill of coaching. Others may simply watch a few YouTube videos, read a book on how to coach, and download the GROW model before heading out to coach. However, working from a credible framework is imperative.

There are countless frameworks and approaches to learning the skill of coaching. Adopting a well-founded framework will help you see the needs of others from a different vantage point - theirs. If you remain attached to your way of thinking and seeing the world, you'll only see their challenges and situations through your lens, and well, it's not YOUR problem it's theirs. So, make sure you're working from a solid and proven framework as your foundation for coaching.

PRACTICE, PRACTICE, PRACTICE.

Imagine before going under anesthesia learning that your surgeon has had little to no surgical practice. Hmmm? Coaching is a practice that requires....practice. Here's the practice framework:

Prepare: breathe, clear your mind, focus on the client.

Practice: by coaching others.

Feedback: gain feedback from the client.

Reflect: what did you learn? How will you improve?

Practice: identify one area for improvement, gain additional development to improve your coaching skills, and then practice some more.

Repeat.

Working with a mentor coach can help significantly. Look for a mentor coach who has more senior coaching experience. Identifying and working with someone who is also in the practice of their own self-development and awareness would be to your advantage.

HOLD YOURSELF ACCOUNTABLE

What type of coach do you want to become? What is the emotional experience you want others to have as a result of their coaching engagement with you? What reputation are you building? How can coaching help? How will you know you've improved and are fulfilling your vision?

All of these are questions we must ask ourselves throughout our journey of development as practice coaches. When you've answered these questions, the final question to ask of yourself:

❓ How will you hold yourself accountable to realize your vision?

....

....

....

....

....

....

....

....

....

....

....

....

....

....

ARE YOU READY?

Establish a Mindset for Coaching

Rushing from meeting to meeting is tempting but will also contribute to a coach who is not focused nor ready for a client who is. Readiness habits to form and practice include:

Center. Give yourself 15 minutes to clear your mind, get centered and prepare for your coaching client.

Breathe. During that time, breathe - take 10 deep breaths, relaxing your body on each exhale, and just relax for a moment.

Hydrate. Are you drinking enough water to remain hydrated? If you want to remain clear-headed, whether you're rushing or not, you'll want to consume the doctor-recommended amount of water each day.

Review. Review briefly any notes from prior conversations with this client. Also, review your practice notes. How might you improve your coaching this time?

Relax. What type of energy do you want to set in the atmosphere? Practice doing what it takes to get there.

Remember, where there is trust, there is no risk. If you want to create an atmosphere and an experience where the client fully places their trust in you, what can you do to mitigate the risk of their trusting you? Rushing into a meeting ill-prepared and without focus is probably not the impression nor experience you want to create.

ARE YOU READY?

Establish a Mindset for Coaching

What needs to change? By when?

....

....

....

....

....

....

....

....

....

....

....

....

....

....

....

....

....

....

....

....

....

....

Masterful Coach Playbook & Journal

QUESTIONS THAT LEAD TO GREATER SELF AWARENESS

I can't say enough about the power of awareness. There's been so much research on it, and coaching centers on the coach's ability to help create awareness because awareness is the beginning of change. If your clients really want change, they will have to do the work.

There is no amount of advising, mentoring, counseling or even coaching that will help someone who isn't willing to embrace the productive discomfort that comes with achieving their goals. It requires the client to be willing to become what researcher, Tasha Eurich, defines as internally and externally aware. In her Harvard Business Review article, **What Self-Awareness Is (and How to Cultivate It)**, we gain a deeper understanding that while most of us think we are self-aware, actually only a small percentage likely are.

[article link: https://hbr.org/2018/01/what-self-awareness-really-is-and-how-to-cultivate-it,]

Internal self-awareness is just that, our own level and degree of awareness of our desires, needs, wants, emotions, thoughts, behaviors, our environment and how we impact others. External self-awareness, therefore, is our own understanding of how each of these things is viewed by others.

Here are a few awareness questions:

- How do you know that to be true?

- What is the emotional impact you want to have on this person, situation, etc.? How will you know when the impact has been met?

- What will be the benefit or reward for you? For them?

- What are you doing now that you were not capable of last year? 3 years ago? 5 years ago?

QUESTIONS THAT LEAD TO GREATER SELF AWARENESS

? Who told you that you can't?

? What's holding you back? What's REALLY holding you back?

? What's the worst that could happen? How will you recover?

? What happened with your last setback? How did you recover? How might that experience serve you today?

? What will happen if nothing changes?

? What needs to happen to move us in a positive direction?

? How much do you care about the experience of the other person? What experience are they having with you? What needs to change? How? When?

And the list goes on and on. Use the space on the next page to journal your list of additional powerful awareness questions and keep them nearby. How will you practice asking deeper awareness questions in your coaching conversations?

MY PERSONAL LIST OF POWERFUL AWARENESS QUESTIONS

....

....

....

....

....

....

....

....

....

....

....

....

....

....

....

....

....

....

....

....

....

....

....

7 MASTERFUL COACHING QUESTIONS

To thoroughly navigate every coaching conversation with ease.

I was joking with a colleague and said, "I can coach you in 7 questions," and she said, "Wait, don't you have a 15-week coach training program? How is that possible?" I replied that the coach training program teaches framework, but the skill comes through practice. Lord knows I've had lots of that. So, the questions here come from years of practice with hundreds of clients over thousands of hours of coaching...practice.

The questions I'm going to share with you assume several things:

✅

You've had a proper intake session with your client and have a clear understanding of their vision and purpose for coaching.

✅

You are prepared to ask follow-up questions throughout as needed.

✅

You know how to get a coaching agreement at the start of each conversation and are attending to the client's goal throughout the session.

✅

You can show flexibility and shift with the client while also attending to their goal.

✅

You can be genuinely curious about someone else and use that curiosity in your coaching.

✅

You're talking less than 20% of the time in the conversation. This conversation is about the client, not your expertise.

7 MASTERFUL COACHING QUESTIONS

No, you don't have to be a certified coach to coach successfully. Training does help to ensure you have a framework to work from and certification gives you greater credibility in a number of ways. We can help with both. Just send us a note to customercare@pamelajgreen.com for information on how you can become a professionally trained and certified coach.

Now you're ready for my list of **7 Masterful Coaching Questions**. Once you've set the atmosphere and have established a trusting relationship with the client, set up the conversation and get started:

1. What do you want to focus on?

2. Why is this important now?

3. What does success look like? What's getting in your way?

4. What behaviors need to change? On a scale of 1-5, how much discomfort are you willing to experience to achieve this goal?

5. What are you going to stop doing? (do more of, etc.)

6. What steps will you take? By when?

7. How will you hold yourself accountable? (who can help, etc.)

As I've stated before, there are quite a few "in-between" questions you can ask for deeper coaching and for clarification. This is not a script, but instead, questions that can guide you to a successful conversation.

JOURNAL YOUR CONVERSATIONS

The remainder of this journal will help with sketching out your conversations. I'm not one to take a bunch of notes as it is a coaching conversation, not a disciplinary one. Too much note taking can make a client very nervous. Coaching is about conversation, not documentation (remember my note on ethics?). Using the GROW model, I've created a space for notes, yes, but just brief notes to write down key points, to stay on track and trigger reminders for future conversations.

GUIDE FOR JOURNALING YOUR CONVERSATIONS

Client Name: Name of Your Client

Session Date: Actual date/time of the session

Session Focus: What has the client indicated they want to discuss (knowing this could change once the session begins). Knowing this helps for planning purposes.

Goal: What is the goal, topic, situation, or challenge the client wants to discuss?

Reality: What's happening? Why is this important now?
This is one of the most important areas of coaching. If you're not coaching in reality, in the present, are you venturing into counseling or some other type of engagement?

Options: What are the options for achieving your goal?
Explore the options at a very basic level if you're not an experienced coach.

Obstacles: What does success look like? What is getting in your way? What behaviors need to change to get you to your vision of the future? How willing are you to experience and work through the discomfort that often comes with change? What might you need to stop doing?
An area often ignored in normal conversations can be powerful in a coaching conversation.

What's Next: Now, what actions/steps will you take? (SMART Goals) Who can help? How will you know you've achieved your goal? How will you hold yourself accountable? When do you want to meet next to discuss your progress?
This is about closing the conversation and inviting self-accountability.

Turn to the back of this journal for more powerful coaching questions.

COACHING CONVERSATIONS

Client Name:

Session Focus:

Session Date: /   /   Session Time:

Goal | What is the goal, topic, situation, or challenge the client wants to discuss?

....

....

....

....

....

Reality | What's happening? Why is this important now?

....

....

....

....

....

Options | What are the options for achieving your goal?

....

....

....

....

....

....

Obstacles | What does success look like? What is getting in your way? What behaviors need to change to get you to your vision of the future? How willing are you to experience and work through the discomfort that often comes with change? What might you need to stop doing?

....

....

....

....

....

....

....

....

What's Next? | Now, what actions/steps will you take? (SMART Goals) Who can help? How will you know you've achieved your goal? How will you hold yourself accountable? When do you want to next meet to discuss your progress?

....

....

....

....

....

....

....

....

....

....

| Follow-on Coaching Session Date | / | / |

COACHING CONVERSATIONS

Client Name:

Session Focus:

Session Date: /   /

Session Time:

Goal | What is the goal, topic, situation, or challenge the client wants to discuss?

....

....

....

....

....

Reality | What's happening? Why is this important now?

....

....

....

....

....

Options | What are the options for achieving your goal?

....

....

....

....

....

....

Obstacles | What does success look like? What is getting in your way? What behaviors need to change to get you to your vision of the future? How willing are you to experience and work through the discomfort that often comes with change? What might you need to stop doing?

....

....

....

....

....

....

....

....

What's Next? | Now, what actions/steps will you take? (SMART Goals) Who can help? How will you know you've achieved your goal? How will you hold yourself accountable? When do you want to next meet to discuss your progress?

....

....

....

....

....

....

....

....

....

....

Follow-on Coaching Session Date   /   /

COACHING CONVERSATIONS

Client Name:

Session Focus:

Session Date: /   /

Session Time:

Goal | What is the goal, topic, situation, or challenge the client wants to discuss?

....
....
....
....
....

Reality | What's happening? Why is this important now?

....
....
....
....
....

Options | What are the options for achieving your goal?

....
....
....
....
....
....

Obstacles | What does success look like? What is getting in your way? What behaviors need to change to get you to your vision of the future? How willing are you to experience and work through the discomfort that often comes with change? What might you need to stop doing?

....

....

....

....

....

....

....

....

What's Next? | Now, what actions/steps will you take? (SMART Goals) Who can help? How will you know you've achieved your goal? How will you hold yourself accountable? When do you want to next meet to discuss your progress?

....

....

....

....

....

....

....

....

....

....

Follow-on Coaching Session Date   /   /

COACHING CONVERSATIONS

Client Name:

Session Focus:

Session Date: /   /

Session Time:

Goal | What is the goal, topic, situation, or challenge the client wants to discuss?

....
....
....
....
....

Reality | What's happening? Why is this important now?

....
....
....
....
....

Options | What are the options for achieving your goal?

....
....
....
....
....
....

Obstacles | What does success look like? What is getting in your way? What behaviors need to change to get you to your vision of the future? How willing are you to experience and work through the discomfort that often comes with change? What might you need to stop doing?

....

....

....

....

....

....

....

What's Next? | Now, what actions/steps will you take? (SMART Goals) Who can help? How will you know you've achieved your goal? How will you hold yourself accountable? When do you want to next meet to discuss your progress?

....

....

....

....

....

....

....

....

....

Follow-on Coaching Session Date   /   /

COACHING CONVERSATIONS

Client Name:

Session Focus:

Session Date: /   /   Session Time:

Goal | What is the goal, topic, situation, or challenge the client wants to discuss?

....

....

....

....

....

Reality | What's happening? Why is this important now?

....

....

....

....

....

Options | What are the options for achieving your goal?

....

....

....

....

....

....

Obstacles | What does success look like? What is getting in your way? What behaviors need to change to get you to your vision of the future? How willing are you to experience and work through the discomfort that often comes with change? What might you need to stop doing?

....

....

....

....

....

....

....

....

What's Next? | Now, what actions/steps will you take? (SMART Goals) Who can help? How will you know you've achieved your goal? How will you hold yourself accountable? When do you want to next meet to discuss your progress?

....

....

....

....

....

....

....

....

....

....

| Follow-on Coaching Session Date | / | / |

COACHING CONVERSATIONS

Client Name:

Session Focus:

Session Date: /   /   Session Time:

Goal | What is the goal, topic, situation, or challenge the client wants to discuss?

....

....

....

....

....

Reality | What's happening? Why is this important now?

....

....

....

....

....

Options | What are the options for achieving your goal?

....

....

....

....

....

....

Obstacles | What does success look like? What is getting in your way? What behaviors need to change to get you to your vision of the future? How willing are you to experience and work through the discomfort that often comes with change? What might you need to stop doing?

....

....

....

....

....

....

....

....

What's Next? | Now, what actions/steps will you take? (SMART Goals) Who can help? How will you know you've achieved your goal? How will you hold yourself accountable? When do you want to next meet to discuss your progress?

....

....

....

....

....

....

....

....

....

....

Follow-on Coaching Session Date   /   /

COACHING CONVERSATIONS

Client Name:

Session Focus:

Session Date: /   /   Session Time:

Goal | What is the goal, topic, situation, or challenge the client wants to discuss?

....

....

....

....

....

Reality | What's happening? Why is this important now?

....

....

....

....

....

Options | What are the options for achieving your goal?

....

....

....

....

....

....

Obstacles | What does success look like? What is getting in your way? What behaviors need to change to get you to your vision of the future? How willing are you to experience and work through the discomfort that often comes with change? What might you need to stop doing?

....

....

....

....

....

....

....

....

What's Next? | Now, what actions/steps will you take? (SMART Goals) Who can help? How will you know you've achieved your goal? How will you hold yourself accountable? When do you want to next meet to discuss your progress?

....

....

....

....

....

....

....

....

....

Follow-on Coaching Session Date   /   /

COACHING CONVERSATIONS

Client Name:

Session Focus:

Session Date: /   /   Session Time:

Goal | What is the goal, topic, situation, or challenge the client wants to discuss?

....

....

....

....

....

Reality | What's happening? Why is this important now?

....

....

....

....

....

Options | What are the options for achieving your goal?

....

....

....

....

....

....

Masterful Coach Playbook & Journal

Obstacles | What does success look like? What is getting in your way? What behaviors need to change to get you to your vision of the future? How willing are you to experience and work through the discomfort that often comes with change? What might you need to stop doing?

....

....

....

....

....

....

....

What's Next? | Now, what actions/steps will you take? (SMART Goals) Who can help? How will you know you've achieved your goal? How will you hold yourself accountable? When do you want to next meet to discuss your progress?

....

....

....

....

....

....

....

....

....

Follow-on Coaching Session Date   /   /

COACHING CONVERSATIONS

Client Name:

Session Focus:

Session Date: /   /

Session Time:

Goal | What is the goal, topic, situation, or challenge the client wants to discuss?

....

....

....

....

....

Reality | What's happening? Why is this important now?

....

....

....

....

....

Options | What are the options for achieving your goal?

....

....

....

....

....

....

Obstacles | What does success look like? What is getting in your way? What behaviors need to change to get you to your vision of the future? How willing are you to experience and work through the discomfort that often comes with change? What might you need to stop doing?

....

....

....

....

....

....

....

....

What's Next? | Now, what actions/steps will you take? (SMART Goals) Who can help? How will you know you've achieved your goal? How will you hold yourself accountable? When do you want to next meet to discuss your progress?

....

....

....

....

....

....

....

....

....

....

Follow-on Coaching Session Date   /   /

COACHING CONVERSATIONS

Client Name:

Session Focus:

Session Date: /   /   Session Time:

Goal | What is the goal, topic, situation, or challenge the client wants to discuss?

....

....

....

....

....

Reality | What's happening? Why is this important now?

....

....

....

....

....

Options | What are the options for achieving your goal?

....

....

....

....

....

....

Obstacles | What does success look like? What is getting in your way? What behaviors need to change to get you to your vision of the future? How willing are you to experience and work through the discomfort that often comes with change? What might you need to stop doing?

....

....

....

....

....

....

....

....

What's Next? | Now, what actions/steps will you take? (SMART Goals) Who can help? How will you know you've achieved your goal? How will you hold yourself accountable? When do you want to next meet to discuss your progress?

....

....

....

....

....

....

....

....

....

| Follow-on Coaching Session Date | / | / |

COACHING CONVERSATIONS

Client Name:

Session Focus:

Session Date: /   /   Session Time:

Goal | What is the goal, topic, situation, or challenge the client wants to discuss?

....

....

....

....

....

Reality | What's happening? Why is this important now?

....

....

....

....

....

Options | What are the options for achieving your goal?

....

....

....

....

....

....

Obstacles | What does success look like? What is getting in your way? What behaviors need to change to get you to your vision of the future? How willing are you to experience and work through the discomfort that often comes with change? What might you need to stop doing?

....

....

....

....

....

....

....

....

What's Next? | Now, what actions/steps will you take? (SMART Goals) Who can help? How will you know you've achieved your goal? How will you hold yourself accountable? When do you want to next meet to discuss your progress?

....

....

....

....

....

....

....

....

....

....

| Follow-on Coaching Session Date | / | / |

COACHING CONVERSATIONS

Client Name:

Session Focus:

Session Date: /   /

Session Time:

Goal | What is the goal, topic, situation, or challenge the client wants to discuss?

....

....

....

....

....

Reality | What's happening? Why is this important now?

....

....

....

....

....

Options | What are the options for achieving your goal?

....

....

....

....

....

....

Masterful Coach Playbook & Journal

Obstacles | What does success look like? What is getting in your way? What behaviors need to change to get you to your vision of the future? How willing are you to experience and work through the discomfort that often comes with change? What might you need to stop doing?

....

....

....

....

....

....

....

....

What's Next? | Now, what actions/steps will you take? (SMART Goals) Who can help? How will you know you've achieved your goal? How will you hold yourself accountable? When do you want to next meet to discuss your progress?

....

....

....

....

....

....

....

....

....

....

| Follow-on Coaching Session Date | / | / |

COACHING CONVERSATIONS

Client Name:

Session Focus:

Session Date: /   /

Session Time:

Goal | What is the goal, topic, situation, or challenge the client wants to discuss?

....

....

....

....

....

Reality | What's happening? Why is this important now?

....

....

....

....

....

Options | What are the options for achieving your goal?

....

....

....

....

....

....

Obstacles | What does success look like? What is getting in your way? What behaviors need to change to get you to your vision of the future? How willing are you to experience and work through the discomfort that often comes with change? What might you need to stop doing?

....

....

....

....

....

....

....

....

What's Next? | Now, what actions/steps will you take? (SMART Goals) Who can help? How will you know you've achieved your goal? How will you hold yourself accountable? When do you want to next meet to discuss your progress?

....

....

....

....

....

....

....

....

....

....

Follow-on Coaching Session Date   /   /

COACHING CONVERSATIONS

Client Name:

Session Focus:

Session Date: /   /   Session Time:

Goal | What is the goal, topic, situation, or challenge the client wants to discuss?

....

....

....

....

....

Reality | What's happening? Why is this important now?

....

....

....

....

....

Options | What are the options for achieving your goal?

....

....

....

....

....

....

Obstacles | What does success look like? What is getting in your way? What behaviors need to change to get you to your vision of the future? How willing are you to experience and work through the discomfort that often comes with change? What might you need to stop doing?

....

....

....

....

....

....

....

....

What's Next? | Now, what actions/steps will you take? (SMART Goals) Who can help? How will you know you've achieved your goal? How will you hold yourself accountable? When do you want to next meet to discuss your progress?

....

....

....

....

....

....

....

....

....

....

| Follow-on Coaching Session Date | / | / |

COACHING CONVERSATIONS

Client Name:

Session Focus:

Session Date: /   /   Session Time:

Goal | What is the goal, topic, situation, or challenge the client wants to discuss?

....

....

....

....

....

Reality | What's happening? Why is this important now?

....

....

....

....

....

Options | What are the options for achieving your goal?

....

....

....

....

....

....

Obstacles | What does success look like? What is getting in your way? What behaviors need to change to get you to your vision of the future? How willing are you to experience and work through the discomfort that often comes with change? What might you need to stop doing?

....

....

....

....

....

....

....

....

What's Next? | Now, what actions/steps will you take? (SMART Goals) Who can help? How will you know you've achieved your goal? How will you hold yourself accountable? When do you want to next meet to discuss your progress?

....

....

....

....

....

....

....

....

....

....

Follow-on Coaching Session Date   /   /

COACHING CONVERSATIONS

Client Name:

Session Focus:

Session Date: /   /

Session Time:

Goal | What is the goal, topic, situation, or challenge the client wants to discuss?

....

....

....

....

....

Reality | What's happening? Why is this important now?

....

....

....

....

....

Options | What are the options for achieving your goal?

....

....

....

....

....

....

Obstacles | What does success look like? What is getting in your way? What behaviors need to change to get you to your vision of the future? How willing are you to experience and work through the discomfort that often comes with change? What might you need to stop doing?

....

....

....

....

....

....

....

....

What's Next? | Now, what actions/steps will you take? (SMART Goals) Who can help? How will you know you've achieved your goal? How will you hold yourself accountable? When do you want to next meet to discuss your progress?

....

....

....

....

....

....

....

....

....

....

| Follow-on Coaching Session Date   /   / |

COACHING CONVERSATIONS

Client Name:

Session Focus:

Session Date: /   /   Session Time:

Goal | What is the goal, topic, situation, or challenge the client wants to discuss?

....

....

....

....

....

Reality | What's happening? Why is this important now?

....

....

....

....

....

Options | What are the options for achieving your goal?

....

....

....

....

....

....

Obstacles | What does success look like? What is getting in your way? What behaviors need to change to get you to your vision of the future? How willing are you to experience and work through the discomfort that often comes with change? What might you need to stop doing?

....

....

....

....

....

....

....

....

What's Next? | Now, what actions/steps will you take? (SMART Goals) Who can help? How will you know you've achieved your goal? How will you hold yourself accountable? When do you want to next meet to discuss your progress?

....

....

....

....

....

....

....

....

....

....

Follow-on Coaching Session Date   /   /

COACHING CONVERSATIONS

Client Name:

Session Focus:

Session Date: /   /   Session Time:

Goal | What is the goal, topic, situation, or challenge the client wants to discuss?

....

....

....

....

....

Reality | What's happening? Why is this important now?

....

....

....

....

....

Options | What are the options for achieving your goal?

....

....

....

....

....

....

Obstacles | What does success look like? What is getting in your way? What behaviors need to change to get you to your vision of the future? How willing are you to experience and work through the discomfort that often comes with change? What might you need to stop doing?

....

....

....

....

....

....

....

....

What's Next? | Now, what actions/steps will you take? (SMART Goals) Who can help? How will you know you've achieved your goal? How will you hold yourself accountable? When do you want to next meet to discuss your progress?

....

....

....

....

....

....

....

....

....

....

| Follow-on Coaching Session Date | / | / |

COACHING CONVERSATIONS

Client Name:

Session Focus:

Session Date: /   /   Session Time:

Goal | What is the goal, topic, situation, or challenge the client wants to discuss?

....

....

....

....

....

Reality | What's happening? Why is this important now?

....

....

....

....

....

Options | What are the options for achieving your goal?

....

....

....

....

....

....

Obstacles | What does success look like? What is getting in your way? What behaviors need to change to get you to your vision of the future? How willing are you to experience and work through the discomfort that often comes with change? What might you need to stop doing?

....

....

....

....

....

....

....

....

What's Next? | Now, what actions/steps will you take? (SMART Goals) Who can help? How will you know you've achieved your goal? How will you hold yourself accountable? When do you want to next meet to discuss your progress?

....

....

....

....

....

....

....

....

....

....

| Follow-on Coaching Session Date   /   / |

COACHING CONVERSATIONS

Client Name:

Session Focus:

Session Date: /   /   Session Time:

Goal | What is the goal, topic, situation, or challenge the client wants to discuss?

....

....

....

....

....

Reality | What's happening? Why is this important now?

....

....

....

....

....

Options | What are the options for achieving your goal?

....

....

....

....

....

....

Obstacles | What does success look like? What is getting in your way? What behaviors need to change to get you to your vision of the future? How willing are you to experience and work through the discomfort that often comes with change? What might you need to stop doing?

....

....

....

....

....

....

....

....

What's Next? | Now, what actions/steps will you take? (SMART Goals) Who can help? How will you know you've achieved your goal? How will you hold yourself accountable? When do you want to next meet to discuss your progress?

....

....

....

....

....

....

....

....

....

....

| Follow-on Coaching Session Date | / | / |

COACHING CONVERSATIONS

Client Name:

Session Focus:

Session Date: /   /

Session Time:

Goal | What is the goal, topic, situation, or challenge the client wants to discuss?

....

....

....

....

....

Reality | What's happening? Why is this important now?

....

....

....

....

....

Options | What are the options for achieving your goal?

....

....

....

....

....

....

Obstacles | What does success look like? What is getting in your way? What behaviors need to change to get you to your vision of the future? How willing are you to experience and work through the discomfort that often comes with change? What might you need to stop doing?

....

....

....

....

....

....

....

....

What's Next? | Now, what actions/steps will you take? (SMART Goals) Who can help? How will you know you've achieved your goal? How will you hold yourself accountable? When do you want to next meet to discuss your progress?

....

....

....

....

....

....

....

....

....

....

Follow-on Coaching Session Date   /   /

COACHING CONVERSATIONS

Client Name:

Session Focus:

Session Date: /   /   Session Time:

Goal | What is the goal, topic, situation, or challenge the client wants to discuss?

....
....
....
....
....

Reality | What's happening? Why is this important now?

....
....
....
....
....

Options | What are the options for achieving your goal?

....
....
....
....
....
....

Masterful Coach Playbook & Journal

Obstacles | What does success look like? What is getting in your way? What behaviors need to change to get you to your vision of the future? How willing are you to experience and work through the discomfort that often comes with change? What might you need to stop doing?

....

....

....

....

....

....

....

....

What's Next? | Now, what actions/steps will you take? (SMART Goals) Who can help? How will you know you've achieved your goal? How will you hold yourself accountable? When do you want to next meet to discuss your progress?

....

....

....

....

....

....

....

....

....

....

Follow-on Coaching Session Date   /   /

COACHING CONVERSATIONS

Client Name:

Session Focus:

Session Date: /   /   Session Time:

Goal | What is the goal, topic, situation, or challenge the client wants to discuss?

....

....

....

....

....

Reality | What's happening? Why is this important now?

....

....

....

....

....

Options | What are the options for achieving your goal?

....

....

....

....

....

....

Obstacles | What does success look like? What is getting in your way? What behaviors need to change to get you to your vision of the future? How willing are you to experience and work through the discomfort that often comes with change? What might you need to stop doing?

....

....

....

....

....

....

....

....

What's Next? | Now, what actions/steps will you take? (SMART Goals) Who can help? How will you know you've achieved your goal? How will you hold yourself accountable? When do you want to next meet to discuss your progress?

....

....

....

....

....

....

....

....

....

....

Follow-on Coaching Session Date   /   /

COACHING CONVERSATIONS

Client Name:

Session Focus:

Session Date: /   /

Session Time:

Goal | What is the goal, topic, situation, or challenge the client wants to discuss?

....

....

....

....

....

Reality | What's happening? Why is this important now?

....

....

....

....

....

Options | What are the options for achieving your goal?

....

....

....

....

....

....

Obstacles | What does success look like? What is getting in your way? What behaviors need to change to get you to your vision of the future? How willing are you to experience and work through the discomfort that often comes with change? What might you need to stop doing?

....

....

....

....

....

....

....

....

What's Next? | Now, what actions/steps will you take? (SMART Goals) Who can help? How will you know you've achieved your goal? How will you hold yourself accountable? When do you want to next meet to discuss your progress?

....

....

....

....

....

....

....

....

....

Follow-on Coaching Session Date   /   /

COACHING CONVERSATIONS

Client Name:

Session Focus:

Session Date: /   /   Session Time:

Goal | What is the goal, topic, situation, or challenge the client wants to discuss?

....

....

....

....

....

Reality | What's happening? Why is this important now?

....

....

....

....

....

Options | What are the options for achieving your goal?

....

....

....

....

....

....

Obstacles | What does success look like? What is getting in your way? What behaviors need to change to get you to your vision of the future? How willing are you to experience and work through the discomfort that often comes with change? What might you need to stop doing?

....

....

....

....

....

....

....

....

What's Next? | Now, what actions/steps will you take? (SMART Goals) Who can help? How will you know you've achieved your goal? How will you hold yourself accountable? When do you want to next meet to discuss your progress?

....

....

....

....

....

....

....

....

....

....

| Follow-on Coaching Session Date | / | / |

COACHING CONVERSATIONS

Client Name:

Session Focus:

Session Date: /   /   Session Time:

Goal | What is the goal, topic, situation, or challenge the client wants to discuss?

....

....

....

....

....

Reality | What's happening? Why is this important now?

....

....

....

....

....

Options | What are the options for achieving your goal?

....

....

....

....

....

....

Obstacles | What does success look like? What is getting in your way? What behaviors need to change to get you to your vision of the future? How willing are you to experience and work through the discomfort that often comes with change? What might you need to stop doing?

....

....

....

....

....

....

....

....

What's Next? | Now, what actions/steps will you take? (SMART Goals) Who can help? How will you know you've achieved your goal? How will you hold yourself accountable? When do you want to next meet to discuss your progress?

....

....

....

....

....

....

....

....

....

....

| Follow-on Coaching Session Date   /   / |

COACHING CONVERSATIONS

Client Name:

Session Focus:

Session Date: /   /

Session Time:

Goal | What is the goal, topic, situation, or challenge the client wants to discuss?

....

....

....

....

....

Reality | What's happening? Why is this important now?

....

....

....

....

....

Options | What are the options for achieving your goal?

....

....

....

....

....

....

Obstacles | What does success look like? What is getting in your way? What behaviors need to change to get you to your vision of the future? How willing are you to experience and work through the discomfort that often comes with change? What might you need to stop doing?

....

....

....

....

....

....

....

....

What's Next? | Now, what actions/steps will you take? (SMART Goals) Who can help? How will you know you've achieved your goal? How will you hold yourself accountable? When do you want to next meet to discuss your progress?

....

....

....

....

....

....

....

....

....

....

| Follow-on Coaching Session Date | / | / |

COACHING CONVERSATIONS

Client Name:

Session Focus:

Session Date: /   /

Session Time:

Goal | What is the goal, topic, situation, or challenge the client wants to discuss?

....
....
....
....
....

Reality | What's happening? Why is this important now?

....
....
....
....
....

Options | What are the options for achieving your goal?

....
....
....
....
....
....

Masterful Coach Playbook & Journal
©2021 Pamela J. Green Solutions, LLC All Rights Reserved Worldwide

Obstacles | What does success look like? What is getting in your way? What behaviors need to change to get you to your vision of the future? How willing are you to experience and work through the discomfort that often comes with change? What might you need to stop doing?

....
....
....
....
....
....
....
....

What's Next? | Now, what actions/steps will you take? (SMART Goals) Who can help? How will you know you've achieved your goal? How will you hold yourself accountable? When do you want to next meet to discuss your progress?

....
....
....
....
....
....
....
....
....
....

Follow-on Coaching Session Date   /   /

COACHING CONVERSATIONS

Client Name:

Session Focus:

Session Date: /   /

Session Time:

Goal | What is the goal, topic, situation, or challenge the client wants to discuss?

....

....

....

....

....

Reality | What's happening? Why is this important now?

....

....

....

....

....

Options | What are the options for achieving your goal?

....

....

....

....

....

....

Obstacles | What does success look like? What is getting in your way? What behaviors need to change to get you to your vision of the future? How willing are you to experience and work through the discomfort that often comes with change? What might you need to stop doing?

....

....

....

....

....

....

....

....

What's Next? | Now, what actions/steps will you take? (SMART Goals) Who can help? How will you know you've achieved your goal? How will you hold yourself accountable? When do you want to next meet to discuss your progress?

....

....

....

....

....

....

....

....

....

....

Follow-on Coaching Session Date   /   /

COACHING CONVERSATIONS

Client Name:

Session Focus:

Session Date: /   /

Session Time:

Goal | What is the goal, topic, situation, or challenge the client wants to discuss?

....

....

....

....

....

Reality | What's happening? Why is this important now?

....

....

....

....

....

Options | What are the options for achieving your goal?

....

....

....

....

....

....

Obstacles | What does success look like? What is getting in your way? What behaviors need to change to get you to your vision of the future? How willing are you to experience and work through the discomfort that often comes with change? What might you need to stop doing?

....

....

....

....

....

....

....

....

What's Next? | Now, what actions/steps will you take? (SMART Goals) Who can help? How will you know you've achieved your goal? How will you hold yourself accountable? When do you want to next meet to discuss your progress?

....

....

....

....

....

....

....

....

....

....

| Follow-on Coaching Session Date | / | / |

COACHING CONVERSATIONS

Client Name:

Session Focus:

Session Date: /   /   Session Time:

Goal | What is the goal, topic, situation, or challenge the client wants to discuss?

....

....

....

....

....

Reality | What's happening? Why is this important now?

....

....

....

....

....

Options | What are the options for achieving your goal?

....

....

....

....

....

....

Obstacles | What does success look like? What is getting in your way? What behaviors need to change to get you to your vision of the future? How willing are you to experience and work through the discomfort that often comes with change? What might you need to stop doing?

....

....

....

....

....

....

....

....

What's Next? | Now, what actions/steps will you take? (SMART Goals) Who can help? How will you know you've achieved your goal? How will you hold yourself accountable? When do you want to next meet to discuss your progress?

....

....

....

....

....

....

....

....

....

| Follow-on Coaching Session Date | / | / |

COACHING CONVERSATIONS

Client Name:

Session Focus:

Session Date: /   /   Session Time:

Goal | What is the goal, topic, situation, or challenge the client wants to discuss?

....

....

....

....

....

Reality | What's happening? Why is this important now?

....

....

....

....

....

Options | What are the options for achieving your goal?

....

....

....

....

....

....

Masterful Coach Playbook & Journal
©2021 Pamela J. Green Solutions, LLC All Rights Reserved Worldwide

Obstacles | What does success look like? What is getting in your way? What behaviors need to change to get you to your vision of the future? How willing are you to experience and work through the discomfort that often comes with change? What might you need to stop doing?

....
....
....
....
....
....
....

What's Next? | Now, what actions/steps will you take? (SMART Goals) Who can help? How will you know you've achieved your goal? How will you hold yourself accountable? When do you want to next meet to discuss your progress?

....
....
....
....
....
....
....
....
....

Follow-on Coaching Session Date   /   /

COACHING CONVERSATIONS

Client Name:

Session Focus:

Session Date: /   /   Session Time:

Goal | What is the goal, topic, situation, or challenge the client wants to discuss?

....

....

....

....

Reality | What's happening? Why is this important now?

....

....

....

....

Options | What are the options for achieving your goal?

....

....

....

....

....

....

Obstacles | What does success look like? What is getting in your way? What behaviors need to change to get you to your vision of the future? How willing are you to experience and work through the discomfort that often comes with change? What might you need to stop doing?

....
....
....
....
....
....
....
....

What's Next? | Now, what actions/steps will you take? (SMART Goals) Who can help? How will you know you've achieved your goal? How will you hold yourself accountable? When do you want to next meet to discuss your progress?

....
....
....
....
....
....
....
....
....
....

| Follow-on Coaching Session Date | / | / |

COACHING CONVERSATIONS

Client Name:

Session Focus:

Session Date: /   /

Session Time:

Goal | What is the goal, topic, situation, or challenge the client wants to discuss?

....

....

....

....

....

Reality | What's happening? Why is this important now?

....

....

....

....

....

Options | What are the options for achieving your goal?

....

....

....

....

....

....

Obstacles | What does success look like? What is getting in your way? What behaviors need to change to get you to your vision of the future? How willing are you to experience and work through the discomfort that often comes with change? What might you need to stop doing?

....

....

....

....

....

....

....

....

What's Next? | Now, what actions/steps will you take? (SMART Goals) Who can help? How will you know you've achieved your goal? How will you hold yourself accountable? When do you want to next meet to discuss your progress?

....

....

....

....

....

....

....

....

....

....

Follow-on Coaching Session Date   /   /

COACHING CONVERSATIONS

Client Name:

Session Focus:

Session Date: / / Session Time:

Goal | What is the goal, topic, situation, or challenge the client wants to discuss?

....

....

....

....

....

Reality | What's happening? Why is this important now?

....

....

....

....

....

Options | What are the options for achieving your goal?

....

....

....

....

....

....

Obstacles | What does success look like? What is getting in your way? What behaviors need to change to get you to your vision of the future? How willing are you to experience and work through the discomfort that often comes with change? What might you need to stop doing?

....

....

....

....

....

....

....

What's Next? | Now, what actions/steps will you take? (SMART Goals) Who can help? How will you know you've achieved your goal? How will you hold yourself accountable? When do you want to next meet to discuss your progress?

....

....

....

....

....

....

....

....

....

....

Follow-on Coaching Session Date   /   /

COACHING CONVERSATIONS

Client Name:

Session Focus:

Session Date: / / Session Time:

Goal | What is the goal, topic, situation, or challenge the client wants to discuss?

....

....

....

....

....

Reality | What's happening? Why is this important now?

....

....

....

....

....

Options | What are the options for achieving your goal?

....

....

....

....

....

....

Obstacles | What does success look like? What is getting in your way? What behaviors need to change to get you to your vision of the future? How willing are you to experience and work through the discomfort that often comes with change? What might you need to stop doing?

....

....

....

....

....

....

....

....

What's Next? | Now, what actions/steps will you take? (SMART Goals) Who can help? How will you know you've achieved your goal? How will you hold yourself accountable? When do you want to next meet to discuss your progress?

....

....

....

....

....

....

....

....

....

Follow-on Coaching Session Date   /   /

COACHING CONVERSATIONS

Client Name:

Session Focus:

Session Date: /   /

Session Time:

Goal | What is the goal, topic, situation, or challenge the client wants to discuss?

....

....

....

....

....

Reality | What's happening? Why is this important now?

....

....

....

....

....

Options | What are the options for achieving your goal?

....

....

....

....

....

....

Obstacles | What does success look like? What is getting in your way? What behaviors need to change to get you to your vision of the future? How willing are you to experience and work through the discomfort that often comes with change? What might you need to stop doing?

....

....

....

....

....

....

....

What's Next? | Now, what actions/steps will you take? (SMART Goals) Who can help? How will you know you've achieved your goal? How will you hold yourself accountable? When do you want to next meet to discuss your progress?

....

....

....

....

....

....

....

....

....

....

| Follow-on Coaching Session Date | / | / |

COACHING CONVERSATIONS

Client Name:

Session Focus:

Session Date: /   /   Session Time:

Goal | What is the goal, topic, situation, or challenge the client wants to discuss?

....

....

....

....

....

Reality | What's happening? Why is this important now?

....

....

....

....

....

Options | What are the options for achieving your goal?

....

....

....

....

....

....

Obstacles | What does success look like? What is getting in your way? What behaviors need to change to get you to your vision of the future? How willing are you to experience and work through the discomfort that often comes with change? What might you need to stop doing?

....
....
....
....
....
....
....
....

What's Next? | Now, what actions/steps will you take? (SMART Goals) Who can help? How will you know you've achieved your goal? How will you hold yourself accountable? When do you want to next meet to discuss your progress?

....
....
....
....
....
....
....
....
....
....

Follow-on Coaching Session Date   /   /

COACHING CONVERSATIONS

Client Name:

Session Focus:

Session Date: /   /   Session Time:

Goal | What is the goal, topic, situation, or challenge the client wants to discuss?

....

....

....

....

....

Reality | What's happening? Why is this important now?

....

....

....

....

....

Options | What are the options for achieving your goal?

....

....

....

....

....

....

Obstacles | What does success look like? What is getting in your way? What behaviors need to change to get you to your vision of the future? How willing are you to experience and work through the discomfort that often comes with change? What might you need to stop doing?

....

....

....

....

....

....

....

....

What's Next? | Now, what actions/steps will you take? (SMART Goals) Who can help? How will you know you've achieved your goal? How will you hold yourself accountable? When do you want to next meet to discuss your progress?

....

....

....

....

....

....

....

....

....

....

Follow-on Coaching Session Date   /   /

COACHING CONVERSATIONS

Client Name:

Session Focus:

Session Date: /   /   Session Time:

Goal | What is the goal, topic, situation, or challenge the client wants to discuss?

....

....

....

....

....

Reality | What's happening? Why is this important now?

....

....

....

....

....

Options | What are the options for achieving your goal?

....

....

....

....

....

....

Obstacles | What does success look like? What is getting in your way? What behaviors need to change to get you to your vision of the future? How willing are you to experience and work through the discomfort that often comes with change? What might you need to stop doing?

....

....

....

....

....

....

....

....

What's Next? | Now, what actions/steps will you take? (SMART Goals) Who can help? How will you know you've achieved your goal? How will you hold yourself accountable? When do you want to next meet to discuss your progress?

....

....

....

....

....

....

....

....

....

....

Follow-on Coaching Session Date   /   /

COACHING CONVERSATIONS

Client Name:

Session Focus:

Session Date: /   /

Session Time:

Goal | What is the goal, topic, situation, or challenge the client wants to discuss?

....

....

....

....

....

Reality | What's happening? Why is this important now?

....

....

....

....

....

Options | What are the options for achieving your goal?

....

....

....

....

....

....

Obstacles | What does success look like? What is getting in your way? What behaviors need to change to get you to your vision of the future? How willing are you to experience and work through the discomfort that often comes with change? What might you need to stop doing?

....

....

....

....

....

....

....

....

What's Next? | Now, what actions/steps will you take? (SMART Goals) Who can help? How will you know you've achieved your goal? How will you hold yourself accountable? When do you want to next meet to discuss your progress?

....

....

....

....

....

....

....

....

....

....

Follow-on Coaching Session Date   /   /

COACHING CONVERSATIONS

Client Name:

Session Focus:

Session Date: /   /   Session Time:

Goal | What is the goal, topic, situation, or challenge the client wants to discuss?

....

....

....

....

Reality | What's happening? Why is this important now?

....

....

....

....

Options | What are the options for achieving your goal?

....

....

....

....

....

....

Obstacles | What does success look like? What is getting in your way? What behaviors need to change to get you to your vision of the future? How willing are you to experience and work through the discomfort that often comes with change? What might you need to stop doing?

....

....

....

....

....

....

....

....

What's Next? | Now, what actions/steps will you take? (SMART Goals) Who can help? How will you know you've achieved your goal? How will you hold yourself accountable? When do you want to next meet to discuss your progress?

....

....

....

....

....

....

....

....

....

....

| Follow-on Coaching Session Date | / | / |

COACHING CONVERSATIONS

Client Name:

Session Focus:

Session Date: /   /

Session Time:

Goal | What is the goal, topic, situation, or challenge the client wants to discuss?

....
....
....
....
....

Reality | What's happening? Why is this important now?

....
....
....
....
....

Options | What are the options for achieving your goal?

....
....
....
....
....
....

Obstacles | What does success look like? What is getting in your way? What behaviors need to change to get you to your vision of the future? How willing are you to experience and work through the discomfort that often comes with change? What might you need to stop doing?

....

....

....

....

....

....

....

....

What's Next? | Now, what actions/steps will you take? (SMART Goals) Who can help? How will you know you've achieved your goal? How will you hold yourself accountable? When do you want to next meet to discuss your progress?

....

....

....

....

....

....

....

....

....

....

Follow-on Coaching Session Date   /   /

COACHING CONVERSATIONS

Client Name:

Session Focus:

Session Date: /   /   Session Time:

Goal | What is the goal, topic, situation, or challenge the client wants to discuss?

....

....

....

....

....

Reality | What's happening? Why is this important now?

....

....

....

....

....

Options | What are the options for achieving your goal?

....

....

....

....

....

....

Obstacles | What does success look like? What is getting in your way? What behaviors need to change to get you to your vision of the future? How willing are you to experience and work through the discomfort that often comes with change? What might you need to stop doing?

....

....

....

....

....

....

....

....

What's Next? | Now, what actions/steps will you take? (SMART Goals) Who can help? How will you know you've achieved your goal? How will you hold yourself accountable? When do you want to next meet to discuss your progress?

....

....

....

....

....

....

....

....

....

....

| Follow-on Coaching Session Date | / | / |

COACHING CONVERSATIONS

Client Name:

Session Focus:

Session Date: /   /

Session Time:

Goal | What is the goal, topic, situation, or challenge the client wants to discuss?

....

....

....

....

Reality | What's happening? Why is this important now?

....

....

....

....

Options | What are the options for achieving your goal?

....

....

....

....

....

....

Obstacles | What does success look like? What is getting in your way? What behaviors need to change to get you to your vision of the future? How willing are you to experience and work through the discomfort that often comes with change? What might you need to stop doing?

....

....

....

....

....

....

....

....

What's Next? | Now, what actions/steps will you take? (SMART Goals) Who can help? How will you know you've achieved your goal? How will you hold yourself accountable? When do you want to next meet to discuss your progress?

....

....

....

....

....

....

....

....

....

....

Follow-on Coaching Session Date   /   /

COACHING CONVERSATIONS

Client Name:

Session Focus:

Session Date: /   /   Session Time:

Goal | What is the goal, topic, situation, or challenge the client wants to discuss?

....

....

....

....

....

Reality | What's happening? Why is this important now?

....

....

....

....

....

Options | What are the options for achieving your goal?

....

....

....

....

....

....

Obstacles | What does success look like? What is getting in your way? What behaviors need to change to get you to your vision of the future? How willing are you to experience and work through the discomfort that often comes with change? What might you need to stop doing?

....

....

....

....

....

....

....

What's Next? | Now, what actions/steps will you take? (SMART Goals) Who can help? How will you know you've achieved your goal? How will you hold yourself accountable? When do you want to next meet to discuss your progress?

....

....

....

....

....

....

....

....

....

| Follow-on Coaching Session Date | / | / |

COACHING CONVERSATIONS

Client Name:

Session Focus:

Session Date: /   /   Session Time:

Goal | What is the goal, topic, situation, or challenge the client wants to discuss?

....

....

....

....

....

Reality | What's happening? Why is this important now?

....

....

....

....

....

Options | What are the options for achieving your goal?

....

....

....

....

....

....

Obstacles | What does success look like? What is getting in your way? What behaviors need to change to get you to your vision of the future? How willing are you to experience and work through the discomfort that often comes with change? What might you need to stop doing?

....

....

....

....

....

....

....

....

What's Next? | Now, what actions/steps will you take? (SMART Goals) Who can help? How will you know you've achieved your goal? How will you hold yourself accountable? When do you want to next meet to discuss your progress?

....

....

....

....

....

....

....

....

....

....

| Follow-on Coaching Session Date   /   / |

COACHING CONVERSATIONS

Client Name:

Session Focus:

Session Date: /   /   Session Time:

Goal | What is the goal, topic, situation, or challenge the client wants to discuss?

....
....
....
....
....

Reality | What's happening? Why is this important now?

....
....
....
....
....

Options | What are the options for achieving your goal?

....
....
....
....
....
....

Obstacles | What does success look like? What is getting in your way? What behaviors need to change to get you to your vision of the future? How willing are you to experience and work through the discomfort that often comes with change? What might you need to stop doing?

....

....

....

....

....

....

....

....

What's Next? | Now, what actions/steps will you take? (SMART Goals) Who can help? How will you know you've achieved your goal? How will you hold yourself accountable? When do you want to next meet to discuss your progress?

....

....

....

....

....

....

....

....

....

....

Follow-on Coaching Session Date   /   /

COACHING CONVERSATIONS

Client Name:

Session Focus:

Session Date: /   /

Session Time:

Goal | What is the goal, topic, situation, or challenge the client wants to discuss?

....

....

....

....

....

Reality | What's happening? Why is this important now?

....

....

....

....

....

Options | What are the options for achieving your goal?

....

....

....

....

....

....

Obstacles | What does success look like? What is getting in your way? What behaviors need to change to get you to your vision of the future? How willing are you to experience and work through the discomfort that often comes with change? What might you need to stop doing?

....

....

....

....

....

....

....

....

What's Next? | Now, what actions/steps will you take? (SMART Goals) Who can help? How will you know you've achieved your goal? How will you hold yourself accountable? When do you want to next meet to discuss your progress?

....

....

....

....

....

....

....

....

....

....

| Follow-on Coaching Session Date | / | / |

COACHING CONVERSATIONS

Client Name:

Session Focus:

Session Date: /   /

Session Time:

Goal | What is the goal, topic, situation, or challenge the client wants to discuss?

....

....

....

....

....

Reality | What's happening? Why is this important now?

....

....

....

....

....

Options | What are the options for achieving your goal?

....

....

....

....

....

....

Obstacles | What does success look like? What is getting in your way? What behaviors need to change to get you to your vision of the future? How willing are you to experience and work through the discomfort that often comes with change? What might you need to stop doing?

....

....

....

....

....

....

....

....

What's Next? | Now, what actions/steps will you take? (SMART Goals) Who can help? How will you know you've achieved your goal? How will you hold yourself accountable? When do you want to next meet to discuss your progress?

....

....

....

....

....

....

....

....

....

....

| Follow-on Coaching Session Date   /   / |

COACHING CONVERSATIONS

Client Name:

Session Focus:

Session Date: /   /

Session Time:

Goal | What is the goal, topic, situation, or challenge the client wants to discuss?

....

....

....

....

....

Reality | What's happening? Why is this important now?

....

....

....

....

....

Options | What are the options for achieving your goal?

....

....

....

....

....

....

Obstacles | What does success look like? What is getting in your way? What behaviors need to change to get you to your vision of the future? How willing are you to experience and work through the discomfort that often comes with change? What might you need to stop doing?

....

....

....

....

....

....

....

....

What's Next? | Now, what actions/steps will you take? (SMART Goals) Who can help? How will you know you've achieved your goal? How will you hold yourself accountable? When do you want to next meet to discuss your progress?

....

....

....

....

....

....

....

....

....

....

| Follow-on Coaching Session Date | / / |

COACHING CONVERSATIONS

Client Name:

Session Focus:

Session Date: /   /

Session Time:

Goal | What is the goal, topic, situation, or challenge the client wants to discuss?

....

....

....

....

....

Reality | What's happening? Why is this important now?

....

....

....

....

Options | What are the options for achieving your goal?

....

....

....

....

....

....

Obstacles | What does success look like? What is getting in your way? What behaviors need to change to get you to your vision of the future? How willing are you to experience and work through the discomfort that often comes with change? What might you need to stop doing?

....

....

....

....

....

....

....

....

What's Next? | Now, what actions/steps will you take? (SMART Goals) Who can help? How will you know you've achieved your goal? How will you hold yourself accountable? When do you want to next meet to discuss your progress?

....

....

....

....

....

....

....

....

....

....

Follow-on Coaching Session Date   /   /

COACHING CONVERSATIONS

Client Name:

Session Focus:

Session Date: /   /   Session Time:

Goal | What is the goal, topic, situation, or challenge the client wants to discuss?

....

....

....

....

....

Reality | What's happening? Why is this important now?

....

....

....

....

....

Options | What are the options for achieving your goal?

....

....

....

....

....

....

Obstacles | What does success look like? What is getting in your way? What behaviors need to change to get you to your vision of the future? How willing are you to experience and work through the discomfort that often comes with change? What might you need to stop doing?

....

....

....

....

....

....

....

....

What's Next? | Now, what actions/steps will you take? (SMART Goals) Who can help? How will you know you've achieved your goal? How will you hold yourself accountable? When do you want to next meet to discuss your progress?

....

....

....

....

....

....

....

....

....

....

Follow-on Coaching Session Date   /   /

COACHING CONVERSATIONS

Client Name:

Session Focus:

Session Date: /   /

Session Time:

Goal | What is the goal, topic, situation, or challenge the client wants to discuss?

....

....

....

....

....

Reality | What's happening? Why is this important now?

....

....

....

....

....

Options | What are the options for achieving your goal?

....

....

....

....

....

....

Obstacles | What does success look like? What is getting in your way? What behaviors need to change to get you to your vision of the future? How willing are you to experience and work through the discomfort that often comes with change? What might you need to stop doing?

....

....

....

....

....

....

....

....

What's Next? | Now, what actions/steps will you take? (SMART Goals) Who can help? How will you know you've achieved your goal? How will you hold yourself accountable? When do you want to next meet to discuss your progress?

....

....

....

....

....

....

....

....

....

....

| Follow-on Coaching Session Date | / | / |

COACHING CONVERSATIONS

Client Name:

Session Focus:

Session Date: /   /   Session Time:

Goal | What is the goal, topic, situation, or challenge the client wants to discuss?

....

....

....

....

....

Reality | What's happening? Why is this important now?

....

....

....

....

....

Options | What are the options for achieving your goal?

....

....

....

....

....

....

Obstacles | What does success look like? What is getting in your way? What behaviors need to change to get you to your vision of the future? How willing are you to experience and work through the discomfort that often comes with change? What might you need to stop doing?

....

....

....

....

....

....

....

....

What's Next? | Now, what actions/steps will you take? (SMART Goals) Who can help? How will you know you've achieved your goal? How will you hold yourself accountable? When do you want to next meet to discuss your progress?

....

....

....

....

....

....

....

....

....

Follow-on Coaching Session Date   /   /

COACHING CONVERSATIONS

Client Name:

Session Focus:

Session Date: /   /   Session Time:

Goal | What is the goal, topic, situation, or challenge the client wants to discuss?

....

....

....

....

....

Reality | What's happening? Why is this important now?

....

....

....

....

....

Options | What are the options for achieving your goal?

....

....

....

....

....

....

Obstacles | What does success look like? What is getting in your way? What behaviors need to change to get you to your vision of the future? How willing are you to experience and work through the discomfort that often comes with change? What might you need to stop doing?

....

....

....

....

....

....

....

....

What's Next? | Now, what actions/steps will you take? (SMART Goals) Who can help? How will you know you've achieved your goal? How will you hold yourself accountable? When do you want to next meet to discuss your progress?

....

....

....

....

....

....

....

....

....

....

Follow-on Coaching Session Date   /   /

COACHING CONVERSATIONS

Client Name:

Session Focus:

Session Date: /   /

Session Time:

Goal | What is the goal, topic, situation, or challenge the client wants to discuss?

....

....

....

....

....

Reality | What's happening? Why is this important now?

....

....

....

....

....

Options | What are the options for achieving your goal?

....

....

....

....

....

....

Obstacles | What does success look like? What is getting in your way? What behaviors need to change to get you to your vision of the future? How willing are you to experience and work through the discomfort that often comes with change? What might you need to stop doing?

....

....

....

....

....

....

....

....

What's Next? | Now, what actions/steps will you take? (SMART Goals) Who can help? How will you know you've achieved your goal? How will you hold yourself accountable? When do you want to next meet to discuss your progress?

....

....

....

....

....

....

....

....

....

....

Follow-on Coaching Session Date   /   /

COACHING CONVERSATIONS

Client Name:

Session Focus:

Session Date: /   /   Session Time:

Goal | What is the goal, topic, situation, or challenge the client wants to discuss?

....

....

....

....

....

Reality | What's happening? Why is this important now?

....

....

....

....

....

Options | What are the options for achieving your goal?

....

....

....

....

....

....

Obstacles | What does success look like? What is getting in your way? What behaviors need to change to get you to your vision of the future? How willing are you to experience and work through the discomfort that often comes with change? What might you need to stop doing?

....

....

....

....

....

....

....

....

What's Next? | Now, what actions/steps will you take? (SMART Goals) Who can help? How will you know you've achieved your goal? How will you hold yourself accountable? When do you want to next meet to discuss your progress?

....

....

....

....

....

....

....

....

....

| Follow-on Coaching Session Date | / | / |

COACHING CONVERSATIONS

Client Name:

Session Focus:

Session Date: /   /   Session Time:

Goal | What is the goal, topic, situation, or challenge the client wants to discuss?

....

....

....

....

....

Reality | What's happening? Why is this important now?

....

....

....

....

....

Options | What are the options for achieving your goal?

....

....

....

....

....

....

Obstacles | What does success look like? What is getting in your way? What behaviors need to change to get you to your vision of the future? How willing are you to experience and work through the discomfort that often comes with change? What might you need to stop doing?

....

....

....

....

....

....

....

....

What's Next? | Now, what actions/steps will you take? (SMART Goals) Who can help? How will you know you've achieved your goal? How will you hold yourself accountable? When do you want to next meet to discuss your progress?

....

....

....

....

....

....

....

....

....

....

| Follow-on Coaching Session Date | / | / |

COACHING CONVERSATIONS

Client Name:

Session Focus:

Session Date: / /

Session Time:

Goal | What is the goal, topic, situation, or challenge the client wants to discuss?

....
....
....
....
....

Reality | What's happening? Why is this important now?

....
....
....
....
....

Options | What are the options for achieving your goal?

....
....
....
....
....
....

Obstacles | What does success look like? What is getting in your way? What behaviors need to change to get you to your vision of the future? How willing are you to experience and work through the discomfort that often comes with change? What might you need to stop doing?

....

....

....

....

....

....

....

....

What's Next? | Now, what actions/steps will you take? (SMART Goals) Who can help? How will you know you've achieved your goal? How will you hold yourself accountable? When do you want to next meet to discuss your progress?

....

....

....

....

....

....

....

....

....

| Follow-on Coaching Session Date | / | / |

COACHING CONVERSATIONS

Client Name:

Session Focus:

Session Date: /   /   Session Time:

Goal | What is the goal, topic, situation, or challenge the client wants to discuss?

....

....

....

....

....

Reality | What's happening? Why is this important now?

....

....

....

....

....

Options | What are the options for achieving your goal?

....

....

....

....

....

....

Obstacles | What does success look like? What is getting in your way? What behaviors need to change to get you to your vision of the future? How willing are you to experience and work through the discomfort that often comes with change? What might you need to stop doing?

....

....

....

....

....

....

....

....

What's Next? | Now, what actions/steps will you take? (SMART Goals) Who can help? How will you know you've achieved your goal? How will you hold yourself accountable? When do you want to next meet to discuss your progress?

....

....

....

....

....

....

....

....

....

....

| Follow-on Coaching Session Date | / | / |

COACHING CONVERSATIONS

Client Name:

Session Focus:

Session Date: /   /   Session Time:

Goal | What is the goal, topic, situation, or challenge the client wants to discuss?

....

....

....

....

....

Reality | What's happening? Why is this important now?

....

....

....

....

....

Options | What are the options for achieving your goal?

....

....

....

....

....

....

Obstacles | What does success look like? What is getting in your way? What behaviors need to change to get you to your vision of the future? How willing are you to experience and work through the discomfort that often comes with change? What might you need to stop doing?

....

....

....

....

....

....

....

....

What's Next? | Now, what actions/steps will you take? (SMART Goals) Who can help? How will you know you've achieved your goal? How will you hold yourself accountable? When do you want to next meet to discuss your progress?

....

....

....

....

....

....

....

....

....

....

Follow-on Coaching Session Date   /   /

COACHING CONVERSATIONS

Client Name:

Session Focus:

Session Date: /   /   Session Time:

Goal | What is the goal, topic, situation, or challenge the client wants to discuss?

....

....

....

....

....

Reality | What's happening? Why is this important now?

....

....

....

....

Options | What are the options for achieving your goal?

....

....

....

....

....

....

Obstacles | What does success look like? What is getting in your way? What behaviors need to change to get you to your vision of the future? How willing are you to experience and work through the discomfort that often comes with change? What might you need to stop doing?

....

....

....

....

....

....

....

....

What's Next? | Now, what actions/steps will you take? (SMART Goals) Who can help? How will you know you've achieved your goal? How will you hold yourself accountable? When do you want to next meet to discuss your progress?

....

....

....

....

....

....

....

....

....

....

| Follow-on Coaching Session Date   /   / |

COACHING CONVERSATIONS

Client Name:

Session Focus:

Session Date: /   /

Session Time:

Goal | What is the goal, topic, situation, or challenge the client wants to discuss?

....

....

....

....

....

Reality | What's happening? Why is this important now?

....

....

....

....

....

Options | What are the options for achieving your goal?

....

....

....

....

....

....

Obstacles | What does success look like? What is getting in your way? What behaviors need to change to get you to your vision of the future? How willing are you to experience and work through the discomfort that often comes with change? What might you need to stop doing?

....

....

....

....

....

....

....

....

What's Next? | Now, what actions/steps will you take? (SMART Goals) Who can help? How will you know you've achieved your goal? How will you hold yourself accountable? When do you want to next meet to discuss your progress?

....

....

....

....

....

....

....

....

....

....

Follow-on Coaching Session Date   /   /

POWERFUL QUESTIONS

What works?

Who else needs to be in the room?

What changes in people skills and behaviors do you think will need to take place?

What is the capacity of our current talent?

What buy, borrow, or build strategies will we apply to acquire the talent needed to achieve our outcomes?

What are the facts?

What do we need to stop doing to focus on this?

What's the big picture here?

What are our choices?

What's useful about this?

What can we learn?

What is the other person thinking, feeling, needing and wanting?

What's possible here?

How does this fit into our service mix, or does it not?

To what extent does the innovation align with our other core competencies?

How can we earn or re-earn everyone's active commiment?

In what ways does this innovation disrupt current activities?

How well does the innovation support the fulfillment of our purpose?

How much risk is associated with this idea? Suggestions to mitigate the risk?

What type of communication strategy shall we adopt for this?

ABOUT THE AUTHOR

Pamela J. Green

Pamela J. Green is an Executive Coach and Consultant who focuses her practice on the development of executives and their teams, advancing executives, and those seeking leadership development. She is a highly sought-after consultant, executive coach, speaker and trainer with more than 30 years of leadership and executive expertise.

Lead Yourself
Lead Others
Lead Your Organization

Pamela and her team excel at equipping current and future executives, their leaders and their organizations with strategies to transform cultures that strengthen employee alignment and activate innovation and creativity. To learn more about our executive coaching and development opportunities:

Connect with Pamela on LinkedIn
www.linkedin.com/in/pamelajgreen

Follow her insights on Twitter
@pamelajgreen

Join her community of leaders at
www.pamelajgreen.com

Get a little more relaxed, and a lot more personal through Facebook:
www.facebook.com/CoachPamelaJCreen

Take our team for a test drive:
customercare@pamelajgreen.com